Discovering My World

Polar Bears

by Melvin and Gilda Berger

T5-CVE-906

SCHOLASTIC INC.

New York Toronto London Auckland
Sydney Mexico City New Delhi Hong Kong

ISBN-13: 978-0-545-16081-0
ISBN-10: 0-545-16081-2

12 11 10 9 8 7 6 5 4 3 2   10 11 12 13 14 15/0

Printed in the U.S.A. 40
First printing, January 2010

Photo Credits:

Cover: © Arco Images GmbH / Peter Arnold, Inc.; Back cover: © Daisy Gilardini / Getty Images; Title page: © BIOS /
Peter Arnold, Inc.; page 3: © Jan Martin Will / Shutterstock; page 4: © Fred Bruemmer / Peter Arnold, Inc.; page 5:
© Keith Levit / Shutterstock; © page 6: © Fred Bruemmer / Peter Arnold, Inc.; page 7: © John Pitcher / iStockphoto;
page 8: © Daniel J. Cox / Corbis; page 9: © Jeff Vanuga / Corbis; page 10: © Jenny E. Ross / Corbis; page 11: © Big Stock
Photo; page 12: © Suzi Eszterhas / naturepl.com; page 13: © Peter Arnold, Inc. / Alamy; page 14: © Daisy Gilardini /
Getty Images; page 15: © Bruce Lichtenberger / Peter Arnold, Inc.; page 16: © John Pitcher / iStockphoto

Polar bears live in the Arctic.

Is the Arctic icy?

The Arctic is a very cold place.

Polar bears like cold places.

What color is the polar bear's fur?

Polar bears have thick fur.

Fur keeps the bears warm.

Polar bears walk on snow and ice.

Do polar bears have furry feet?

Their flat feet are like snowshoes.

Can polar bears swim underwater?

Polar bears like to swim.

Polar bears like to dive, too.

What are their dens made of?

Polar bears make dens in winter.

Cubs are born in the dens.

What is the mother bear doing?

Polar bear mothers take care of their cubs

The cubs stay close to their mothers.

Ask Yourself

1. Where do polar bears live?
2. Is the Arctic cold?
3. Can polar bears walk on ice?
4. Where are polar bear cubs born?
5. Are polar bears good mothers?

You can find the answers in this book.